C000141208

© **Michael Scott 2020**

Printed in the United States of America

Contents

WordPress Installation in Root Directory

Detailed steps to Install and Setup WordPress in Root Directory through your Domain Control Panel

WordPress Theme Installation and Other Functions

How to Install and Activate New Theme on your WordPress Website

Installation of Plugins

How to Install Elementor Plugin to your WordPress

How to Install Astra Plugin in WordPress

Step by Step Guide on How to Create Posts with Elementor

How to make yours Posts Appear First on your Website

How to build Pages with Elementor and Menus Creation

Deleting Existing Pages in WordPress

How to Build a Real Estate Website with Elementor

How to Add the Pages to Navigation Menu as Items

How to Build Construction Website with Elementor Page Builder

What you must have Completed before this Stage

Step by Step Guide in Creating Pages for a Construction company Website

Creating the Home Page

Creating the "WHAT WE DO" Page

How to Create the WHO WE ARE page

Building PROJECTS and NEWSROOM Pages

Building Website with Elementor Pro 3.0 Beta

How to Access your Elementor Theme Builder

The Components of the Theme Builder

Chapter 1

Introduction to WordPress and Elementor

Building websites with elementor page builder is a way of spicing up website pages. It is a trend that has been ongoing for about two years now. Elementor has really made webpages look excellent and appealing to the eyes.

In the past, we, website builders, could not complete any website page without the use of codes. These include HTML and CSS codes. With the coming of WordPress, we began to do many things on our own without writing any form of complicated codes.

Of a truth, with the development of WordPress Content Management System, a complete website can be built within 30 minutes. I mean a website that will function in a standard way. It is an introduction made possible by great minds. Their introduction of WordPress sends us message which means "you people should stop cracking your brains on the tags and elements to use to write codes for websites."

In institutions of higher learning, students of computer science, computer engineering and any study relating to computer software still learn codes. They are taught that because it is the basic of computer and its operation. But when they finished learning these codes, some that will go into the field of website building and development will find it easier.

They will find out that what they will do in the real-world pertaining website building is much easier. It is so because of the handwork of WordPress. They have done all the coding at the background. That is as a result of the work done by the team of great minds.

Elementor as a company adds their own contributions to make building with WordPress easier. With elementor page builder, you are left with the option to choose any templates of your choice to build websites. There are specific templates that are best for any kind of website. You will find out more with time.

WordPress and Elementor Explained

If you are a beginner, you might have been hearing WordPress frequently every time among website builders. You may even think deeper on how it came about. Without taking much of your time, WordPress is a Content Management System used to create websites. It is the building block of many websites.

WordPress is not the only Content Management System that you can use to build websites. There are others Content Management Systems which among them is Joomila. Irrespective of the availability of the other Content Management Systems, 37.6% of all websites used on the web are created with WordPress. WordPress is the simplest, most popular way to create websites or blogs. WordPress was released for the first time on May 27, 2003.

Elementor is new introduction to WordPress to beautify websites created with WordPress. It is a unique introduction made available to give WordPress created websites unique designs. There are free and pro elementor page builders. The pro elementor page builders are not free. If you want to use such page builder, you have to pay. Quoting from Elementor website, "Elementor is a page builder plugin that replaces the basic WordPress editor with a live frontend editor, so you can create complex layouts visually, and design your website live, without having to switch between the editor and the preview mode".

Updates in the Version of Elementor Plugins used in WordPress

Notwithstanding the fact that elementor plugin has helped in building sophisticated websites, updates are being made frequently to make sure that it works properly. These updates made on the plugin improves its function and reducing any error that may occur while building with this plugin. I started writing this book section on August 27, 2020 and then there was a release of new elementor version for both the free version and the pro. The version was Elementor V 3.0 Beta for Pro version and 3.0.1 for the free version. This version of elementor is shown in the figure below as it appeared on my WordPress dashboard.

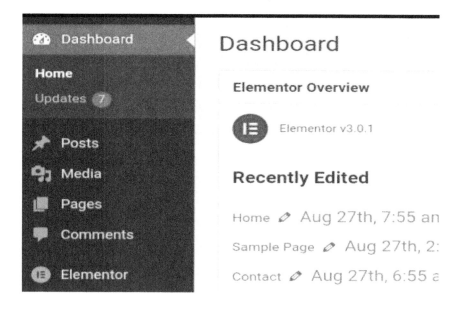

Fig 1: Picture shows Elementor 3.0.1 for elementor free version

What's New in Elementor 3.0 Beta Pro version

In the new Elementor 3.0 Beta Pro version released by Elementor company in the recent time, there are new added features.

These added features in the elementor plugin are as follow:

- Design System Features

- New Theme Builder, and

- Significant Performance Improvements.

With the design system features, you can Manage your site's design system from one place. It is a good development because you can do different things from one particular "house" with this feature. I will carryout this practically when I start building websites with elementor plugin.

The new Theme Builder is a powerful visual tool for managing every part of your website without code. It is a nice improvement worthy of being praised. The company did a great job in development of this feature. I love the feature.

In terms of significant performance improvements, this feature is exceptional. Nobody will like to build any website page that does not load fast. Even you as a reader of this book will not be happy to find yourself in a sluggish website. This is because you need time to do other things concerning your life and not just being on one website page for long.

With the improvement in significant performance, the company with her team of developers worked hard to maintain fast page loading speed. When you open any webpage built with elementor page builder, the page loads fast due to this improvement. With this, your website is ranked high among others due to its fast loading.

What kind of Websites can be Built with Elementor?

Elementor can be used to build different kinds of websites. I have built different websites with classy look using this plugin. The kinds of websites you can build with elementor are but not limited to:

- Blog sites

- Portfolio websites

- Real estate

- Café

- Restaurant

- News

- Construction

- Brochure

- E-commerce

- Education

- Infopreneur

- Organization and

- Fitness websites

Elementor has many templates that fit into any kind of website you want to build. It gives you room to build any kind of websites you want to build to your taste. It is a replica of innovation.

Are All Templates on Elementor Free to be used?

No. Not all templates on elementor are free to be used. You need to pay before you can make use of the templates to build some sites.

Let me inform you, Elementor is not just a company that was opened to run free services for people. It is also a business company. Elementor Ltd. is an Israeli software company. The company built elementor plugin that we can use to build good looking websites. It was founded in the year 2016.

So, before you can import and use some templates on your

website, which is from elementor plugin, you are to pay. When you pay to have such template, Elementor and WordPress make money. That is one of the reasons for the collaboration between the two companies.

If you are "falling in love" with a particular template on elementor and you found out that it is not free as it is tagged "Agency", just try and pay for it. It is not too bad to pay because such kind of template was built under someone's sweat. So, try and pay if you really want to use such template on your website.

You can pay as low as $49 and you become upgraded to Elementor Pro. In fact, you have many more advantages in Elementor Pro version. There are many more functions you can perform through it. But if you cannot pay, just choose other free templates available.

Chapter 2

Domain Name and Website Hosting

The first thing to do while building a website is to choose and register a domain name. A domain name is the name which your website will answer. It is unique name and no other website on the web bears same domain name.

You can decide to have your domain name as smartreading for example. What this implies is that after creating the website, when people type www.smartreading.com, they will be taken to your website. So that name smartreading is unique and no other person can have that same smartreading as a domain name.

If you are building an author's website for instance, you can choose a domain name that is like your author's name. For example, the name of an author Michael Scott can have a domain name michaelscott. What it means is that when people visit a website www.michaelscott.com, that author's website page will open.

Choosing a Domain Name

As earlier explained, a domain name is a unique name. It is your website name. A domain name is the address where internet users can access your website. In choosing any domain name, there are things you have to know.

What you need to Know before Choosing a Domain Name

To choose a domain name, it is important to take note of the following:

(1) Choose a domain name that is simple and unique

(2) Choose the name that people can easily remember

(3) Your domain name should be short and not a full sentence

(4) Only numbers, alphabets and hyphen are allowed in domain name

(5) Special characters, examples $,&,# are not accepted in domain name.

Hosting with a Domain Name Registrar

No matter any country you find yourself, there are many domain name registrars that can allow you host your domain under them. It is a domain name registrar that will register any domain name you want to use and make sure that the site is active on the web. Because there are many approved domain name registrars, you have your choice to choose from any of them. So, when I said that irrespective of any country you find yourself you can register your domain name, it is a clear message. You do not need to visit their offices to get your domain name registered, which you will use to build a full website. Everything is happening online so you can register your domain name online and pay with your debit or credit card. It is just as simple as ABC.

In some countries, there are some domain name registrars that specifically operate there and have more customer-base over there. If you want to host your website with the domain name registrars that operate more effectively locally, you can make your research on that. But to me, you do not need to pass through the stress of asking around as there are some domain name registrars which are known globally for their outstanding works. These are companies that have made names for themselves. All you need is to fill an online form with them and choose the name you want your website to answer, and within 12 hours your website becomes active.

What Functions do Domain name registrars Cover?

A domain name registrar is a business that handles the reservation of domain names as well as the assignment of IP (Internet Protocol) addresses for those domain names. The functions of domain name registrars are as follow:

(1) They make sure that your domain name (your website name) is registered

(2) They make sure that your website files are stored in their server

(3) Domain name registrars work always to make sure that your website is active on the internet so that when people visit your website URL they can find the content on it.

(4) Domain name registrars make ICANN (Internet Corporation for Assigned Names and Numbers) know about your existing website and hence make your website get approval to feature on the internet.

How many Websites can you Host with a Domain Name Registrar?

You can host as many websites as you want with any domain name registrar. You can choose to host with one particular domain name registrar, or you can try any other company that still offer the same service. Domain name registrars are business companies so they will be happy to see you register more websites with them so that they will make more money. It is all about business so feel free to do more business with them.

Website Hosting Companies

There are many website hosting companies/domain name registrars that you can host a website with. They are unique in their ways and their hosting prices vary. The lists of website hosting companies are as follow:

Bluehost

Dreamhost

HostGator

Hostinger

A2 Hosting

GreenGeeks

WP Engine

InterServer

WordPress Hosting

Inmotion

SiteGround and

WestHost

These are just the few website hosting companies among many others. So, you can visit any of the companies' websites, check for the availability of the domain name you want to answer. After, pay for that domain name and hosting and start building your website. I will break these steps down to you as we proceed.

How to host your Website with Bluehost

In this section, I will be teaching you how to host your website with Bluehost. Over 2 million websites are powered by Bluehost today. The website hosting company is doing well, and it has been recommended by many users to others.

Let me throw a little light on the term "hosting" before we proceed deeper into this subheading. Hosting is a service that allows organizations and individuals to post a website or web page onto the Internet. A web host, or web hosting service provider, is a business that provides the technologies and services needed for the website or webpage to be viewed on the internet.

I will be teaching you on how to host your website using Bluehost but know that you can use any other website hosting company to set up your website. You can choose of those website hosting companies I mentioned or any website hosting company you like that was not listed by me.

Step by Step Guide in Hosting a Website with Bluehost

To host your website with Bluehost, these steps are what you need to take

Step 1

Visit the website of the company via the company URL (www.bluehost.com)

Fig 2: The homepage of Bluehost showing the website URL

Step 2

Click on the **Get Started** button and choose any plan of your choice.

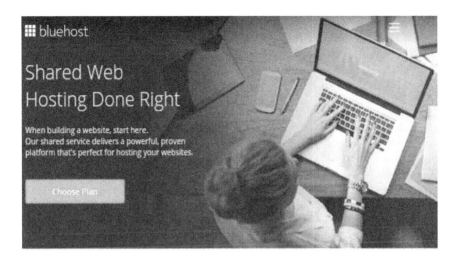

Fig 2.1: Plans offered by Bluehost and the different prices

There are many plans available on Bluehost website. The plans vary depending on some factors. The factors include the disk space you need, the band width, the kind of server you need (whether dedicated or shared server) and other factors.

Step 3

Select any plan from the list of plans offered by Bluehost by clicking on the **Select** button.

Step 4

From the next page that will open, type the name of the domain you want your website to answer and Click on **Next**. For example, I can type "learntech20" to check if the domain name is free. If it is free, you will see notification on the next page telling you it is free. But if it is not, you will still be shown a notification on that.

Fig 2.2: Page to check for domain name availability

Step 5

Fill the form

Fill in your contact information, your debit or credit card information in the next page, and also information of the site you want to host with the company. As you fill the online form, deselect any service ticked by Bluehost by default to reduce the total cost you will pay for the hosting. But if you are building a "big company's" website, you can leave that to strengthen the security of the website.

19

Step 6

Click on "**Submit**" button to submit the information you filled for the hosting. You will be required to choose a password for your account with Bluehost. You can decide to accept auto password generation or you can choose to create your password yourself. If you are creating the password by yourself, please make your password strong. You can create the password in such a way that it contains letters, numbers and special characters. Doing so will make your password strong and not easy to be broken into. Also save your password in a place that people cannot have access to it easily.

Step 7

Payment Confirmation

Once the payment for your domain and hosting is successful, you will receive email on that. The email will contain basic information on your registration and how-to login to the control panel of your domain.

Addition information may be requested from you for your domain registration with ICANN. Remember that ICANN stands for Internet Corporation for Assigned Names and Numbers.

WordPress Installation in Root Directory

In this section I will be teaching you on steps to install WordPress Content Management System to your domain. It is after the installation and setup that you can proceed to other sections that will allow you to start building your website using elementor page builder and other tools.

Detailed steps to Install and Setup WordPress in Root Directory through your Domain Control Panel

Step 1

Login to Your Domain Control Panel

After the payment of your domain has been confirmed and you are sent confirmation message along with the details you need to login to your domain Control Panel, then login.

First, you have to click on the control panel link sent to you for the login page to open. After that, insert the login username and the password sent to you to login to your control panel.

As you successfully login, a new page open. This new page shows some functions. These functions are much but we will work with those that concern us in this teaching.

Fig 2.3: The page that opens as you login to domain C Panel**Step 2**

Locate the **SOFTACULOUS APPS INSTALLER** Section

Inside the control panel, search for the section that bears the subheading **SOFTACULOUS APPS INSTALLER** and you will see some Content Management Systems Applications there. Examples are WordPress and PrestaShop under **Scripts**.

The location of this section can vary depending on the host control panel you are making use of. If you hosted your domain with Bluehost, you will find this under "**MOJO Marketplace**". So, when you get to this section just choose "**One-Click Installs**". Under it you will see some software which among them is **WordPress**.

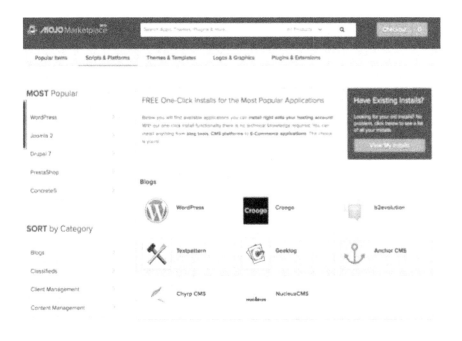

Fig 2.4: Software under MOJO Marketplace including WordPress

Step 3

Click and install WordPress

Click on WordPress under **SOFTACULOUS APPS INSTALLER** or **One-Click** Installs and then install the software.

Step 4

Setup the Installed WordPress

You are expected to fill in the basic information in the form that opens.

The form is divided into sections. The sections are "Software Setup", "Site Settings", "Admin Account", Language Selection and Theme Selection sections.

Under **Software Setup** section, in the "**In Directory**" that has "**wp**" inside, delete the "**wp**" for the box to be empty. This will make WordPress to be installed to the root Directory of the domain.

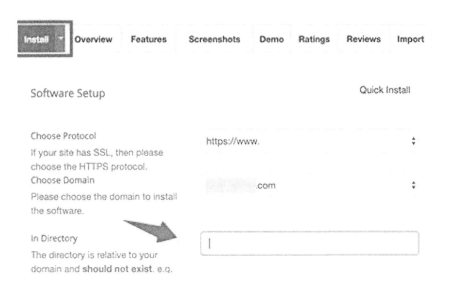

Fig 2.6: Always leave the "In Directory" empty as shown

In the "**Choose Domain**" type the name of your domain. For example, I have to type in "learntech20" if that is my domain name.

Under "**Site Settings**" fill the necessary information needed. Do not enable **Multisite** if not necessary. In the "**Site Settings**" section, fill in the basic information about your website. This includes the main title of your website and its subheading. For example, I can decide to use **Learn Tech 2020** in the site title section. I can briefly explain the site in the other box.

Follow this similar way to fill the other information needed in the other section. Put the email address you want to use to receive your installation details in the last rectangular box provided. After going through the information, you filled and believe everything is correct, just click on the "**Install**" button. Once the installation is successful, you will see a congratulatory message and link to login to WordPress.

Chapter 3

WordPress Theme Installation and Other Functions

There are many themes available on WordPress that you can use to build your websites. WordPress has many themes that can fit in to different kinds of websites. Also, there are some themes that are best when used with elementor plugin. Among them is Astra and Hello elementor theme. So, you can choose any among the two.

In Chapter 2, I discussed how to Install WordPress Content Management System app to the root directory of your domain. I believe you were able to complete that task successfully. In this chapter, I will be teaching you on how you can choose a new theme irrespective of the theme you selected when you installed WordPress through the control panel.

A theme is used to simplify the process of creating a website. It is a collection of templates and stylesheets that define the appearance and display of a website. A theme comes with different design layouts, and that is why many website builders keep changing themes until they see the one they feel fits into the kind of website they are building. Themes have their individual unique features.

How to Install and Activate New Theme on your WordPress Website

The first thing you should do after installing and setting up your WordPress through the control panel of your domain is to install a new WordPress theme that will help you design your new website. I recommend that you install a theme called Astra or Hello elementor. The reason for this recommendation is because elementor page builder works well with any of them since the topic is on "WordPress and Elementor"

To install and activate WordPress theme, take the following procedures:

(1) Login to your WordPress dashboard

If you can remember, when you finished setting up your WordPress through the control panel of your domain, you were shown a link through which you could use to login to your WordPress admin dashboard. My own for example in this teaching is www.learntech20.com/wp-admin. So, in the same line, replace my own domain name (learntech20) with your own domain name and then enter it in a browser search space, and search.

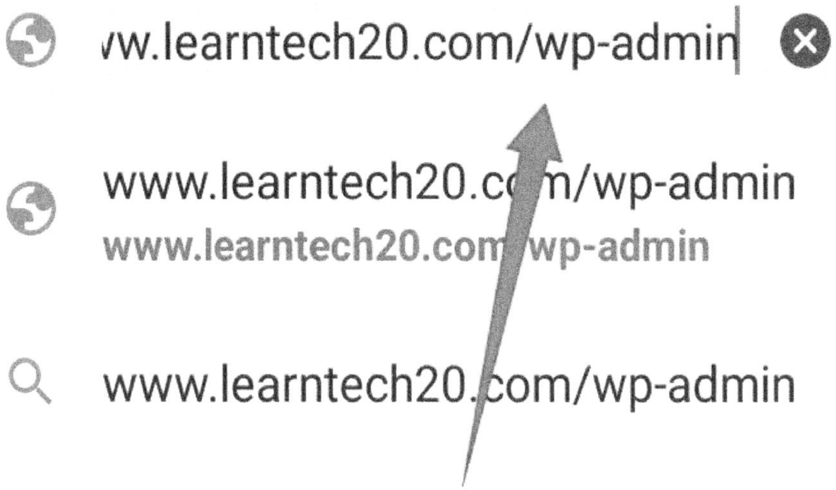

vw.learntech20.com/wp-admin ✖

www.learntech20.com/wp-admin
www.learntech20.com/wp-admin

www.learntech20.com/wp-admin

Fig 3: Entered WordPress account admin URL in a browser.

(2) Enter your username and password to login to your WordPress admin dashboard

As you entered your admin URL and hit search as I explained to you in step 1, a new page opens requesting for your **username/email** and **password**, type in the requested details. What is needed is the username/email and the password you entered when you were setting up your WordPress account through your domain control panel.

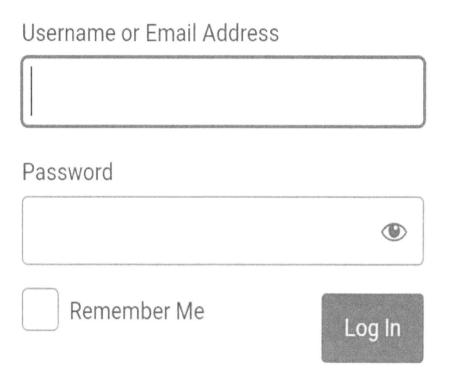

Fig 3.1: Enter the username or email and password and click on log In

(3) Select **Appearance** from the screen options as you login

(4) Select **Themes**

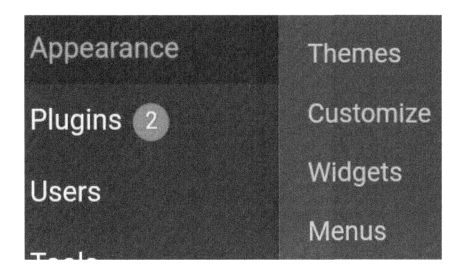

Fig 3.2: Select Appearance and then Themes

(5) Click on **Add New**

(6) In the search box that opens, type **Astra** and Astra theme will show up

(7) Click on it, click **Install** and then **Activate** button to activate the theme

With these steps, you are done with new theme installation on your website.

Installation of Plugins

To successfully build stunning websites using WordPress and elementor page builder, you have to install the necessary plugins. In fact, elementor page builder is a plugin so we have to install it in order for us to be able to work with it. A plugin is a software that can be uploaded to WordPress Content Management System to extend and expand the functionality of websites built with WordPress.

Other major plugins we need to build websites with elementor are elementor, Astra plugin (because in this teaching am building the website using Astra theme) and elementor header and footer plugins. You have to make sure you install these major plugins to make your design easy. One of the reasons you need to install Astra plugin is because this plugin also come with additional template builders. As a result of this, if you are building your website with free elementor page builder, some templates elementor will not give you free, Astra plugin will do that for you.

How to Install Elementor Plugin to your WordPress

To install elementor plugin in your WordPress, take the following steps:

Step 1

Login to your WordPress admin dashboard using your email and password

Step 2

Select **Plugins** screen option among others

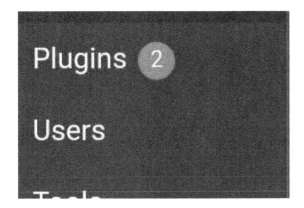

Fig 3.3: Plugins screen option shown above

Step 3

Select **Add New**

As you click on **Add New** button, a new page opens for you to search for the plugin you need which is elementor

Step 4

Type **elementor page builder** in the search box

In the plugin search box that allows you to search for any plugin you want to install on your WordPress, just type elementor page builder and the plugin will show up. Ensure you are on search by keywords option and not by author's/developer's name.

Step 5

Install and Activate the plugin

As the elementor page builder plugin shows up, click on the **Install Now** button followed by **Activate** which will show up after you clicked on **Install Now**

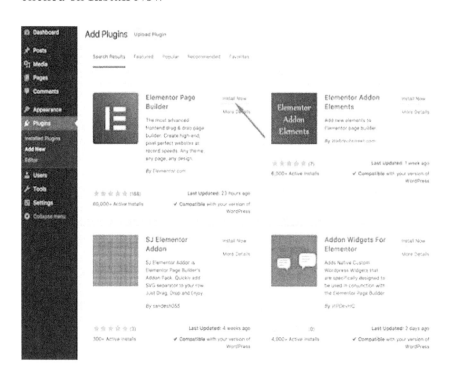

Fig 3.4: Installation of elementor page builder

At this point you are done with complete installation and activation of elementor page builder plugin. So elementor will work well at this stage in building of your website.

How to Install Astra Plugin in WordPress

As earlier stated, since we are using Astra theme in this teaching, we will be needing Astra plugin as well. Astra plugin will make us have larger template library. So, we are left with the option to either choose template builder from Astra or elementor. Astra plugin works hand-in-hand with elementor.

To install Astra plugin, you have to take the following steps:

Step 1

Login to your WordPress admin dashboard

Step 2

Select **Plugins** screen option

Step 3

Select **Add New**

As you select Plugins as stated in step 2, some functions are displayed, so you are to select **Add New** among them.

Step 4

Type in Astra in the search box

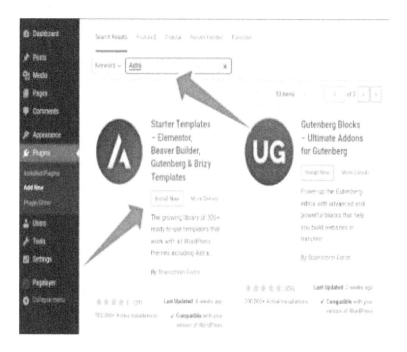

Fig 3.5: Installation of Astra plugin

Step 5

Click on Astra as it shows up among many other plugins

Step 6

Install and Activate

As the plugin shows up, just click on **Install Now** button followed immediately by **Activate**. Once the activation is successful, you will see a notification on that.

Step by Step Guide on How to Create Posts with Elementor

Posts are important elements of every website. If you are building a blog site with WordPress and elementor collaboration, it is important to know how to create posts with elementor. The reason for this is because publishing posts is your priority in building this type of website. I want to inform you that those things you were able to do by just creating and publishing your posts with only WordPress, you can still do it and much more with elementor page builder.

In this section, I will be taking you on step by step illustration on how to create and publish posts on your website using elementor. It is easy to follow guide. Please I will leave my email address on the last page of this book so you can write to me if you encounter any challenge in this teaching. I will always respond to your mail because I want you to succeed.

To create post using elementor through your WordPress account, take the following steps:

Step 1

Login to your WordPress admin account

Using your username/email and password for your WordPress account, just login to the admin account.

Step 2

Click on the **Posts** screen option and then select **Add New** button as well

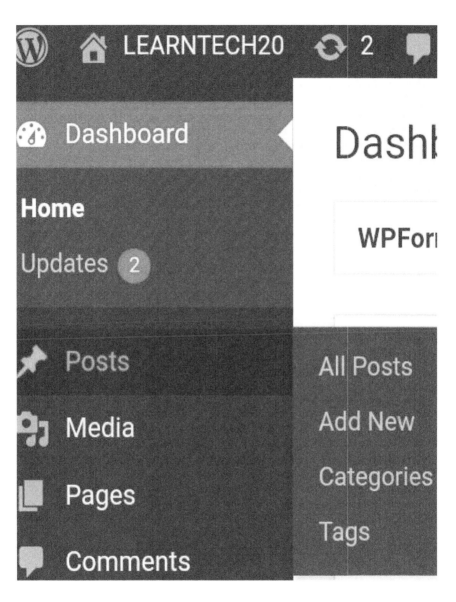

Fig 3.6: You are to select Posts followed by Add New

Step 3

Enter the title of your post in the title box provided for you

Step 4

Compose the body of your article inside the body section of the word editor made available by WordPress.

Step 5

After you are done writing your articles, look at the top part of that page where you are and select **Edit with Elementor** tab

When you do that, elementor will load and open. Do not be in a rush, just allow it to open completely to enable you complete some tasks.

Step 6

You can further write and add some other elements in your posts

On that elementor environment, you can add some elements or contents to that your post. For example, you can add images to that your post before you published it. Just go to that your article and click on it and select the pen-like button and edit the content.

When you click on the content section to start your editing, a text editor environment open. You can also add images by clicking on the image icon on the text editor.

Fig 3.7: Text editor opened as I tried to edit with elementor

You can also decide to add quote about the author at the bottom part of the article after writing the post. You can select any block template from the template section. There are many things you can do.

Step 7

Click on **Publish** button to publish your post

After writing and beautifying your post, just click on **publish** at the bottom part of the environment to publish your article.

How to make yours Posts Appear First on your Website

Sometimes beginners' intention by building websites with WordPress and elementor is usually to create blogs that will attract many readers. As a result of this, they want their posts to appear first once visitors visit their sites. In this section, I will be teaching you on how you can make your posts appear first to the eyes of your readers irrespective of the fact that you have homepage which by default should be the first page your website visitors are to see.

Step by Step Guide on how to make Posts appear First on your Website

To carry out this easy task, take the following steps

Step 1

Login to your WordPress admin dashboard

Step 2

Select **Settings**

Among the screen options that you will see when you login to the dashboard of your WordPress, just select **Settings**. This option is among the last if not the last.

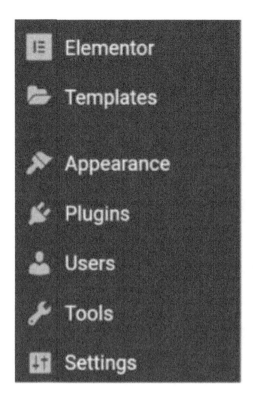

Fig 3.8: Settings screen option comes after Tools as shown in this picture

Step 3

Select **Reading** option

Step 4

In the section "**Your homepage Displays**" select "**Your latest**

44

Posts"

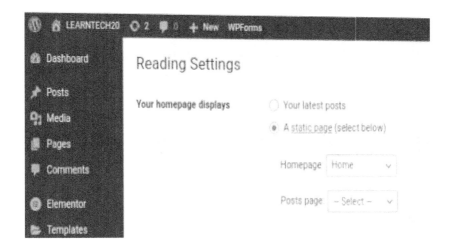

Fig 3.9: Select the box of "Your latest posts" instead of "Static page"

Step 5

Click on **Save Changes** button

Click on the **Save Changes** button to save the change in your settings. The **Save Changes** button is on the bottom right-hand site of the same page. Once you do this, you are done with this task. If you visit your website homepage from that time up, it will show you latest published posts. For example, if I visit www.learntech20.com after I made this change, I will see my latest posts on my website.

Chapter 4

How to build Pages with Elementor and Menus Creation

This is an important title to learn something new in the field of WordPress and elementor. I will be taking you on ways you can use to create new pages using elementor page builder. These methods are two and I will be taking you on the two. But the two methods are easy to follow and apply. If you encounter any difficulty in doing this, do not hesitate to write to me. My email is at the last part of this book. I want you to get it right at the end, so feel free to write to me. The reason you bought this book on elementor is to learn something in that area and I want you to understand it properly.

On the other hand, menus are needed in a website that is built to target readers. Through the menus, a reader that wants to read only one post on your website ends up reading more than 10 pages. And you know what that mean? The higher the number of pages he read, the higher the chance of getting more clicks. When I say clicks, I mean clicking on adverts placed on that website which gives you money in return. If the website is an e-commerce website, the higher the pages or products viewed, the more chances you have to make more sales.

If you have taken a good look on a website like amazon.com, you will notice that are many pages that are added to the footer menu of the website. Do you know why they added so many pages as menu items at the footer menu? It is because they want people that visit the website to access other websites or links where they can be directed to. Some when directed to the pages or links end up buying more items. And as they make such purchases, Amazon and the company makes money. It is a marketing strategy.

Fig 4: The footer menu items of amazon.com

In this section, I will be teaching you how these footer items that are available on amazon.com were added. I will start from page creation and after that I will take you on how to create footer menu. And finally, on how the created pages are added to the footer menu to form footer items.

Deleting Existing Pages in WordPress

When you installed new WordPress themes, some of them usually come with already created pages. In this subheading, I will be teaching you on how you can delete the pages that come with the theme your installed in your WordPress.

To delete the already existing pages in your WordPress, take the following steps:

Step (1)

Login to your WordPress dashboard

Step (2)

Select **Pages** from the list of the screen options

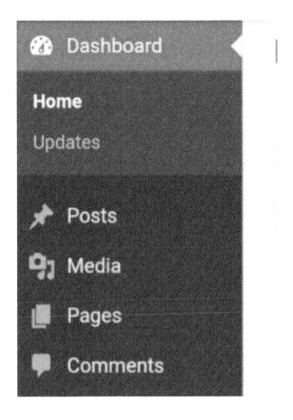

Fig 4.1: Select Pages among all the screen options

Step (3)

Select All Pages

As you click on Pages, sub options show up which among them is all pages. Just click on the **All Pages**

Step (4)

Tick all the pages and select **Trash** action to delete all of them from WordPress.

Step by Step Guide on how to build New Pages with Elementor Through Admin Dashboard

You can build new pages you want your website to operate with using elementor page builder. In this section I will be teaching you on how to use free elementor page builder to create new pages that can fit into websites in easy to follow guide. The pages I will be teaching you how to build using elementor through WordPress admin dashboard are:

- Home and
- About

How to build the Home Page

To build the Home page of a website for example blog site using elementor page builder through WordPress dashboard, take the following steps:

Step 1

Login to your WordPress admin Dashboard

Using your WordPress administrator link, username or email address and password, login to your WordPress account.

Step 2

Select **Pages** screen option

Step 3

Select **Add New**

As you select the **Add New** button, WordPress word editor environment will open

Step 4

Type in the name of the page in the title section

Since I am building a page named **Home** in this section, I will type **Home** in that space

Step 5

Select **Edit With Elementor**

Edit With Elementor button is at the top right-hand corner of the page. So, select it for elementor page builder environment to open.

Fig 4.2: **Edit with Elementor** button pointed at by the arrow

Step 6

Start your Design

As the elementor page builder environment opens, there are a lot of things you can do. You can use drag and drop approach to pick any element you like and drop it on any part of the design environment. For example, you can drag and drop the text header element and have it on the design environment. Make the necessary change you want to make.

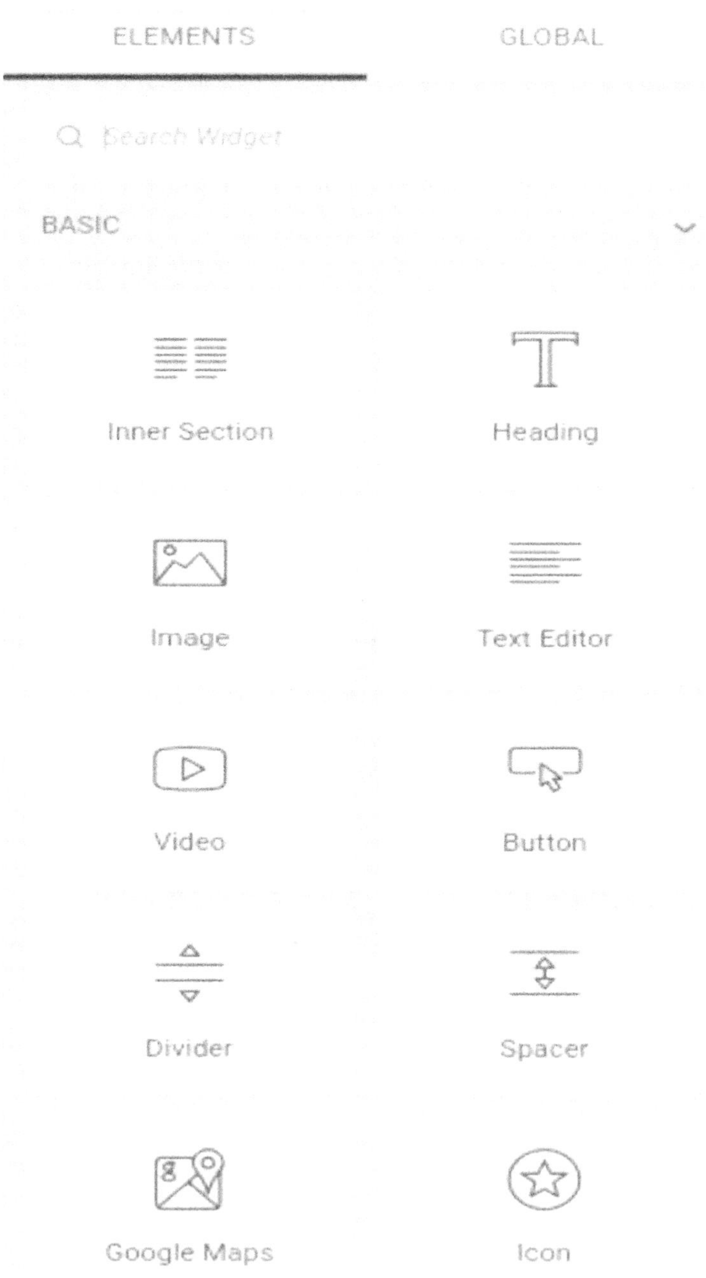
ELEMENTS
GLOBAL
Search Widget
BASIC
Inner Section
Heading
Image
Text Editor
Video
Button
Divider
Spacer
Google Maps
Icon

Fig 4.3: Some elementor elements that you can use for your

website page design

Step 7

Import a template from the template library

Since I installed both Astra and elementor plugins in this teaching, I am left with the option to either import page builder template with either elementor or Astra. So, you can choose to import templates from any of them.

At the bottom part of the design environment, click on either the page builder with symbol "A" or the one with folder-like design for the template library to be opened.

Fig 4.4: Select from any of the two to have access to template library

As you select any of them, a new window opens which shows you

55

some page templates. Some of these templates are free while others are not. If you are building with free elementor plugin, you have to pay before you can use those templates that have **Agency** tagged on them.

Fig 4.5: Template library of elementor page builder

Using the search box by the top right-hand corner of the template library, type in the name of the template you need. For example, you can type the word "blog" and some blog temples will be shown to you.

You can click on any of the templates you like among the list. Sometimes when you click on any of them, you are shown sub parts of that template. This can be "**Home", "About", "Contact" and "Service"**. You can choose the Home because we are building a **Home** page. But if it is **Contact**, you then choose contact sub template part.

Also, since we are building the homepage of the website in this teaching, you can type in "Home" in the search box and home templates will display. From there you can make your choice. Click on any of the templates you like and select **Import**. This will make the template to be imported to the page.

Step 8

Edit the imported template and save

The imported page builder comes with default pictures and words on it. You can edit these pictures and words to your own taste. For the text, take your cursor to the part you want to make changes on, click on that part and some functions will show up. Among them is the pen-like design. Click on that pen-like button, delete the words you do not like and replace them with yours. You can even delete any module you do not like. You can click on the default pictures you do not like on the page builder and then replace them with your own pictures.

Step 8

Click on **Publish** button to save changes

When you finish editing the page, just click on the green **publish** button to save your changes.

Fig 4.6: The position of **Publish** button at bottom left-hand corner

You can still visit the page later if you want to make further changes on it. Just click on any part of the page you want to edit; delete some words you do not like and replace them with your own. You can also use drag and drop technique to add elements and any picture you want. After your editing, click on **Update** button which now replaces the place of **Publish** button initially used.

How to Create "About Page" using Elementor through WordPress Admin Dashboard

In the same approach I taught you how to create and build Home page using elementor page builder, you can create and build **About page**. **About page** is a page that informs readers of your website what the website is all about. In this section, I will quickly teach you how you can create and build this page using elementor page builder.

To create and build the About page through your WordPress administrator dashboard, take the following steps:

Step 1

Login to your WordPress admin dashboard with your email/username plus your password

Step 2

Select **Pages** screen option followed by **Add New** immediately

Step 3

In the title section of the word editor, type **About**

Step 4

Click on **Edit with Elementor** located at the top left-hand corner of the WordPress word editor

Step 5

Select either the **Astra** symbol or the **folder** design for a new window to open for you to choose any template of your choice.

Step 6

Use the search box to get the right template

As the template library opens, you are left with the choice of many available templates made available by elementor. Since you are building **About** page, you can type **About** in the search box located by the right. That will show you some About templates.

On the other hand, you can streamline your search to free templates if you want to build with such templates only. By the left-hand top side, there is a dropdown. This allows you to choose search condition of templates. You can just choose **Free** and then choose from the free available templates.

If you make your search with words like blog or article for instance, you will be shown the templates in that category. When you click on any of them, you will be shown subcategories like **Home, About, Contact, Projects, and Services**. Since you are building **About** page, select the one pre-built with the name About.

Step 7

Import and edit the template

As you selected the template, just click on **Import** button to have the template introduced on your about page. Make the necessary changes you need to make.

Step 8

Hit the **Publish** button to get the page published

As you finish editing your template to the standard you want it, just click on the **Publish** button. Once you do this, you page becomes published on your site and visible to the whole world.

You can use these same steps to create as many pages as you want.

Another Approach you can use to create and Build Pages with Elementor

There is another approach you can use to create and build your website pages using elementor page builder for the pages. In this section, I will be teaching you on this. Though it is not so different from the one I just taught you on, but it is important you know about it. In this method, you start the page creation through your website and not through mainly from the admin dashboard.

Step by Step Guide on How to Create and Build Pages Through the Website Using Elementor

In this section, I will be teaching you on easy to follow guide on building a page through your website. You can build any kind of page through this approach. Here, I will be focusing on how to create a **Contact** page only.

To create the **Contact** page through this approach, take the following steps:

Step 1

Log in to your WordPress dashboard using your WordPress login details

Step 2

Open a new tab in that same browser you are using and visit your website URL (Your main site link)

Example is visiting the website URL am using for this teaching, www.learntech20.com. So, you are to visit yours.

Step 3

Select the **+New** sign on top of the website and some options will be displayed

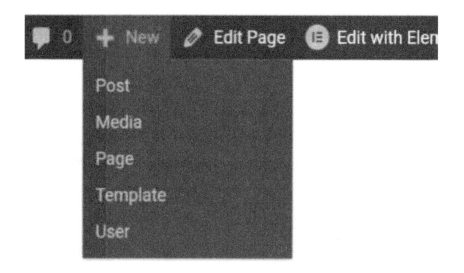

Fig 4.7: Some options that will display as you select the +**New** **sign**

Step 4

From the options that displays, click on **Page**

Step 5

Enter the title of the page in the title section and then click on **Edit with Elementor**

As you select the Page as shown in Fig 4.7, WordPress word editor environment opens. Just enter the name of the page in the title space. Since am building **Contact** page in this particular teaching,

I have to write **Contact** in that space. Then click on **Edit with Elementor** at the top right-hand corner.

Step 6

On the elementor environment, look at the bottom left-hand corner and click on the gear symbol which is the settings of the elementor.

When you click on the settings, at the **Page Layout** section, select **Elementor Full Width** from the dropdown.

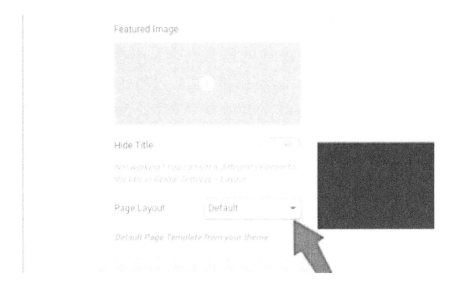

Fig 4.8: Selecting Elementor Full Width

Step 7

Click on the Astra or folder sign for the template library to open

Step 8

Using my previous guide, search for any template that is made for contact page, click on it and import it to your contact Page.

Step 9

Edit the imported template to fit your page. Delete the existing contact information by default and add that of yours or that of the client you are building the website for. You can also drag and drop any element you like from page builder elements options from the left-hand side.

Step 10

Click on **Publish** button

When you click on **Publish** button, the page you built becomes published. You can use this approach to build other pages of your choice. It is a complete easy to follow guide.

Step by Step Guide in Creating menus and Adding Pages to the Menus

I will first teach you how to create main menu first before the footer menu. Also, I will guide you through on how to add our already created pages to the menu.

Step by Step Guide on how to create Main Menu

By default, many themes come with main menu already created. But if the theme you are using do not have the main menu, then create it by taking the following steps:

Step 1

Login to your WordPress admin dashboard using your login details

Step 2

Select **Appearance** screen option follow immediately by **Menus**

When you select the Menus tab, the menu editor opens.

Fig 4.8: The menu editor that will open when you click on **menus**

Step 3

Click on **Create a new menu** button

Step 4

Type in the name of the menu. Since I am teaching you how to create Main Menu, type in **Main Menu** as the menu name

Step 5

Click the **Create Menu** button. Once you click on that **Create Menu** button, the Main Menu is created.

Step 6

Add the pages you want to have as your menu items

Look at the left-hand side and you will see the existing pages on the website. Select all the pages you want to add at the main menu by ticking the boxes. Select Add to menus and those pages will be added as menu items on your website.

Step 7

Save the menu and the items

Click on the **Save Menu** button, the menu and the added items will be saved.

Step by Step Guide in Creating Footer Menu and Adding it to the Site

This is another area I will take you on. I this section, I will take you on step by step guide on how to create Footer Menu and how to add them to display on the bottom (footer) section of your websites. You can build footer menus with the names Footer Menu, Footer 1, Footer 2, and Footer 3. The individual footer menu will have different pages in it as footer items. At the end, they are lined up at the footer area of the website. This is how amazon.com website has many pages at the footer part of the website as shown in Fig 4.

The steps to create footer menu is not different from the one I taught you on how to create main menu. In summary, to create footer menu and add pages as footer items, take the following steps:

Step 1

Login to your WordPress admin dashboard using your login details

Step 2

Select **Appearance** screen option follow immediately by **Menus**

When you select the **Menus** tab, the menu editor opens.

Step 3

Click on **Create a New menu** button

Step 4

Type in the name of the menu. Since I am teaching you how to create Main Menu, type in **Footer Menu** as the menu name

Step 5

Click the **Create Menu** button. Once you click on that **Create Menu** button, the Footer Menu is created.

Step 6

Add the pages you want to have in your footer menu items

Look at the left-hand side and you will see the existing pages you have created. Select all the pages you want to add at the **footer menu** by ticking the boxes. Select **Add to menus** and those pages will be added as footer menu items on your website.

Step 7

Save the footer menu and the items

Click on the **Save Menu** button and the menu and the added items (pages) will be saved.

How to Add the Footer Menu to the Footer Section of your Website

Be it a website you are building for your use or for a client, there are simple steps you can take to add the already created footer menu which contains pages as the footer items to your website. This will establish more readership on your website. To add the footer menu, take these steps:

Step 1

Login to your WordPress admin dashboard

Step 2

Click on **Appearance** which is among WordPress screen options

Step 3

Click on **Customize**

Step 4

Select **Menus**

Among all the options that will display when you click on Customize, just select Menus

Step 5

Select **Footer Menu**

The Footer Menu is the Footer Menu I created which contains some pages as the menu items.

Step 6

Under **Menu locations**, tick "**Footer Menu**" box

When you tick on this box, this will remind the system that you want the menu to be placed at the footer area of the website

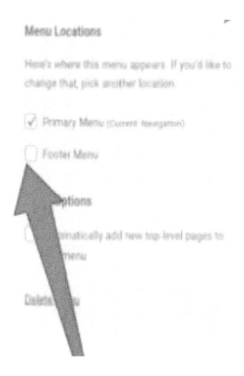

Fig 4.9: The footer menu box to be selected shown

From the picture, you have to tick that **Footer Menu** box and uncheck that of **Primary Menu**

Step 7

Click on **Publish** button

Depending on the theme you are using, the **Publish** button can be on the top or bottom part of the menu section. Just click on it and your footer menu containing pages as items will be made available on your website.

You can visit your website and see the contents of the footer section. If you click on any of them, for example **Contact**, you will be taken to the full **contact** page to read what is contained on the page.

With this my teaching, I believe you understood something great.

Chapter 5

How to Build a Real Estate Website with Elementor

In this Chapter, I will be teaching you on how to build a functioning real estate website. This is a step by step guide that will help you learn something good on real estate site building. I am giving you this teaching with elementor free templates building process.

Elementor has many templates that can help you build nice real estate websites. Few of these templates are free while many are not free to use. What it means is that you have to upgrade your elementor plugin to pro version if you do not like the free templates. But the free templates are not bad in any way. You can change the default images that come with the template to the main pictures you want to use.

This teaching can be called a standalone topic because I am

teaching you on how to build a real estate website using WordPress Content Management System and Elementor template for the design. In this chapter's teaching, I assume that you have hosted your website through any website hosting company, **installed WordPress on the root directory of the domain through control panel, installed and activated Astra theme and Astra plugin, and also installed and activated elementor plugin**.

The template I will be teaching you with may have an e-commerce application. What I mean is that the template may show homes and furniture with price attachments which visitors to the site can click on to pay for the products, and the products delivered to the address they filled.

You can decide to delete that part to disable online purchase. But you can decide to allow it. If you want it to be active and be functioning on the real estate website you have to build it with elementor ecommerce template which requires the need for installing WooCommerce plugin.

In this teaching, I will not cover the e-commerce activation on building real estate website. But I can recommend a book for you on that. You can buy a book titled "Beginners Guide to Building E-Commerce Websites" by William S. Page. You will learn something good from there. But I will cover the basic guide on how to build real estate company website in this chapter without involving ecommmerce activation.

What you must have Understood before this Stage

In this Chapter, I assume that you have known how to do the following:

(1) How to Create Pages

(2) How to add the created Pages to the main menu as menu items.

Step by Step Guide in Choosing Real Estate Template

The steps needed to get this task done is as follow:

Step 1

Sign into you WordPress Admin area

You are to use your username or email address plus your password to sign in.

Step 2

Open a new browser and visit your website link

Using the website address am using in this teaching which only works for this teaching period, I will visit www.learntech20.com.

Step 3

Create a Page with elementor and Choose a real estate template

As you are on your website already, what you are to do next is to create a page. This page will stand as your homepage first before creating other pages like Store, Service, Contact, and About Us.

To create the page, first you are to select the + **New** sign on top of your website and then pages. This is for you to be able to add a new page that will form your homepage.

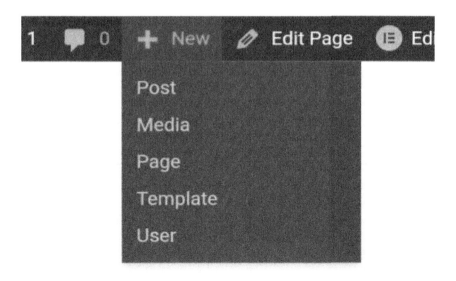

Fig 5: Select **Page** as shown on the website

On the page that open, type in name in the title section. For example, you can write "**Home**" in the space. Click on **Edit with Elementor**. A new page will then open.

In the new page that opens, click on the gear icon (Settings) at bottom and at **Page Layout** select **Elementor Full Width**.

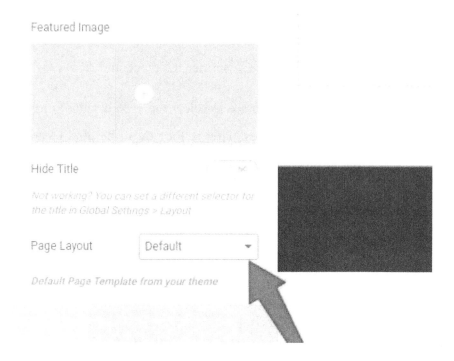

Fig 5.1: Choosing Elementor Full Width

Next, click on the Astra plugin symbol so that you will be allowed to choose a template.

Fig 5.2: Astra plugin symbol pointed at by the arrow

In the Search box that is under pages template, type in **Real estate** and some templates will show up. Choose the free one among the template if you are using free elementor plugin. But if you are using pro, you can choose the one with agency tagged on it.

Among the real estate templates that will be shown by the search result, I recommend you choose the one with the name "**Real Estate-Home**". Click on the template and select **Import Template** that will appear on the top. After the importation, the template loads.

Find Your Perfect Home

🏠 Residential

🏠 Residential

Modern Apartment

Family Home

$ 1500/mo

$ 175,000

3 bd / 2 ba / 1100 Sq Ft

4 bd / 3 ba / 2700 Sq Ft

🏢 Commercial

🏢 Commercial

Modern Apartment

Elegant Studio Flat

$ 2000/mo

$ 138,000

3 bd / 3 ba / 1450 Sq Ft

3 bd / 2 ba / 1100 Sq Ft

Fig 5.3: Part of the newly imported real estate elementor template

You can then start making the changes you want on the template. When you are satisfied with the design you have, just click on **Publish** to save your changes. You can come back to the same page to add more beauty on the design. After you are done with the changes, just hit on **Update** to save your new changes.

With this guide, you can create other pages that will make up the website. You can create pages like Blog, About, Contact, Store, and Team. It is a simple task to carryout.

How to Add the Pages to Navigation Menu as Items

To add your created pages to the main menu, which is also known as the navigation menu, follow this quick guide via character:

Login to your website admin area> Appearances> Menus> Navigation Menu or Main Menu> Click the boxes for the pages you want to add> Add to Menu> Arrange the pages in the ways you want them to be in drag and drop approach> Save Menu.

With these simple and straight forward guides, you will add the pages to the main menu.

Chapter 6

How to Build Construction Website with Elementor Page Builder

There are many construction companies from different parts of the world that need well-designed sophisticated websites. These construction companies are ready to pay good amount of money to website builders so far, they get what they want from the designer.

Instead of writing series of codes for a long time which you know can report errors in coding as you go into your design, elementor page builder has made it easy for us. There are free and purchasable templates available on elementor plugin that you can use for this building. One of the good things about this method is that you can edit the template you want to use after importing it to WordPress. What you can do with elementor page builder is endless.

The process to get this task completed is the same with that explained in chapter 5. Where the difference comes in is when you want to choose the template for the building of the website. At this stage, instead of choosing real estate template, you go for construction template. At the end, you edit the entire template to suite what you want. I will be taking you on how to get this task done in step by step guide.

What you must have Completed before this Stage

For the purpose of time saving and avoidance of repeating some processes again, there are some tasks I believe you have completed before now. These tasks are as follow:

(1) How to Host a Website

I taught you how to host a website with any website hosting company in chapter 2 of this book. There are many website hosting companies you can host your website with. They are, but not limited to GoDaddy, Bluehost, InterServer, HostGator, SiteGroud, and DreamHost.

When you host your website with any of these website hosting companies, they make sure that your site is always online. Also, they take it upon themselves to store your website files on their server. A website hosting company helps your website to be live. More on how to host a website is in Chapter 2.

(2) You have Setup your Site and Installed WordPress Theme on your Website

I also discussed how you can set up WordPress in the root directory of your domain in chapter 2 of this book. On a quick way, you can do this by logging into the control panel of your domain using the link given to you by your website hosting company. After that, you go to the App section, install WordPress and set it up through the control panel.

For the WordPress theme installation, you do that when you login to the admin area of your WordPress. I advice you Install Astra theme. That will make it easier for us to work with. Read more on theme installation in chapter 2.

(3) You must have Installed Astra Plugin and Elementor Plugin

I previously taught you on how you can install and activate Elementor and Astra plugin. In summary, to install these plugins, take these steps:

- Login to your WordPress admin area

- Select Plugins

- Select Add New

- Type in the name of the plugin you want to install inside the search box, example elementor

- Click on the plugin, install and activate it

What you must have known how to do before now

Before now, I expect you to know how to create pages and how to add them to the main menu items of your website. Though I will still touch it here, I expect that you have learned how to do them from my previous teaching in this book. You can create pages when you **login to your admin area, choose the pages option from the dashboard and the Add new.** From there you can build the page with elementor by choosing the option of **Edith with Elementor**.

Another way is by logging into your WordPress admin area, then visit your website in a new tab of the same browser, click on the + **New** and select Pages. With this, you edit with elementor and then get the task completed with other few steps.

Step by Step Guide in Creating Pages for a Construction company Website

In this section, I will be teaching you on how you can create pages for the Construction company website. The pages I will be teaching you on how to create are as follow:

(1) HOME

(2) WHAT WE DO

(3) WHO WE ARE

(4) PROJECTS and

(5) NEWSROOM

I am using the design employed by **Bechtel construction company of United States** to give you this teaching. The picture of the pages that were added as the menu items of the website is shown below.

Fig 6: The items that make up the main menu of Bechtel

89

construction company

So, I will be teaching you on how to build a construction company website that will look like that of Bechtel construction company of United States using elementor page builder plugin.

The HOME page of the website will contain some basic information and activities of the company. It can contain brief information of the company, recent projects, testimonies of clients, and the team of workers of the company.

The other pages will contain the information that relates to the title of the individual page.

Creating the Home Page

To create the **Home Page** of the construction company Website, you can take these steps

(1) Login to your WordPress dashboard

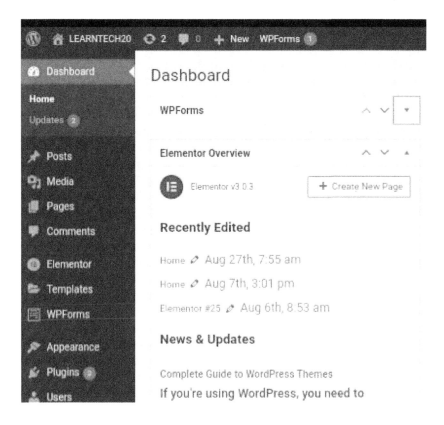

Fig 6.1: My WordPress Admin dashboard

(2) Select **Pages** and followed by **Add New**

(3) Type in the name of the Page as **Home** in the title section

(4) Select **Edit with Elementor**

(5) Locate the **settings** at the bottom left corner and click on it

(6) In the **Page Layout** select the dropdown button and click on **Elementor Full Width**

(7) Click on the **Astra – like** (designed with symbol A) symbol for a new page to open to search for construction template

91

Fig 6.2: The Astra-like symbol

(8) Make sure it is on **Page** heading and type **Construction** in the search box to search for the template

(9) Among the many templates that will show up, choose the one you like. When I was designing, I chose the one that has the heading as "**Broad Vision**…." When you click on it, you will be shown some other sub-templates that makes up the design.

All ▼

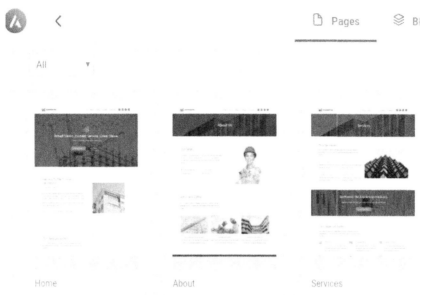

Home   About   Services

Fig 6.3: The sub-templates of the template I chose

(10) Since you are building the home page of the construction company, select the one with the name **Home** at the bottom. Click on the **Import Template** button. After the importation is completed, start your editing.

(11) Move your cursor to any part of the page you want to edit, click on that part, delete what you do not want, add your own words, drag and drop pictures from your personal computer. Any module you do not like, click on the **"X"** button to delete it. When you are satisfied with what you have, click on the "**Publish**" button by the button left corner to save your changes. Elementor has made things easy for we website builders.

93

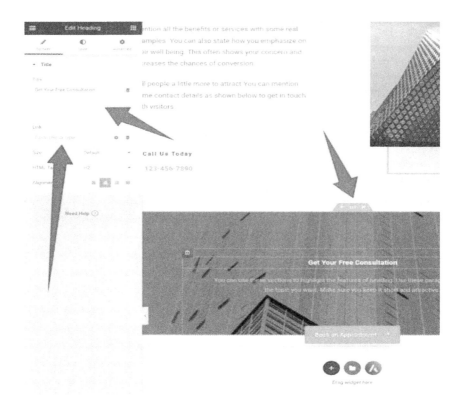

Fig 6.4: Quick illustration on how you can make changes on the template

From the figure above I was trying to explain how you make changes to any part of the page after the importation of the construction template. When you are on any part of the page, it shows what you can do on the page. For example, if you click on the + sign as shown above, it shows some functions that you can select to add either new page builder or block. Also, in the illustration, I was about changing the words "**Get Your Free Consultation**" to my own words. You will find it fun when you try it.

Creating the "WHAT WE DO" Page

In this section, I will be teaching you on how to create the second page in the list of pages which I named **WHAT WE DO** page. It is the same process that I taught you on how to create **HOME** page. To create this page, still take these steps:

(1) Login to your WordPress dashboard

(2) Select **Pages** and followed by **Add New**

(3) Type in the name of the Page as **WHAT WE DO** in the title section

(4) Select **Edit with Elementor**

(5) Locate the settings at the bottom left corner and click on it

(6) In the **Page Layout** select the dropdown button and click on **Elementor Full Width**

(7) Click on the **Astra – like** (designed with symbol A) symbol for a new page to open for search for construction template

(8) Make sure it is at **Page** heading and type **Construction** in the search box to search for the template

(9) Among the many templates that will show up, choose the one you like. When I was designing, I chose the one that has the heading title as "**Broad Vision**...." When you click

on it, you will be shown some other sub-templates that makes up the design.

(10) Since you are building the **WHAT WE DO** page of the construction company, select the one with the name **Services** at the bottom. Click on the **Import Template** button. After the importation is completed, start your editing.

(11) Move your cursor to any part of the page you want to edit, click on that part, delete what you do not want, add your own words, drag and drop pictures from your personal computer. After you finish with your editing, just save your work by hitting the **Publish** button.

LEARNTECH20

Fig 6.5: The WHAT WE DO page

In the above picture, I changed the original words on the top of the page to **WHAT WE DO**. What was there before was **Services**.

How to Create the WHO WE ARE page

Just like the way I created the two pages using elementor page builder, you can still create the **WHO WE ARE** page in the same way. This kind of page just explains the company. It is just like the **About Us** page we see as menu items on many websites. So, you can just import any **About Us** page from the elementor page builder library, redesign it and use it on your construction company website.

To achieve this task, take the following steps:

(1) Login to your WordPress dashboard

(2) Select **Pages** and followed by **Add New**

(3) Type in the name of the Page as **WHO WE ARE** in the title section

(4) Select **Edit with Elementor** which is on top of the page

(5) Locate the settings at the bottom left corner and click on it

(6) In the **Page Layout** select the dropdown button and click on **Elementor Full Width**

(7) Click on the **Astra – like** (designed with symbol A) symbol for a new page to open to search for construction template

97

(8) Make sure it is at **Page** heading and type **Construction** in the search box to search for the template

(9) Among the many templates that will show up, choose the one you like. When I was designing, I chose the one that has the heading title as "**Broad Vision**...." When you click on it, you will be shown some other sub-templates that makes up the design.

(10) Since you are building the **WHO WE ARE** page of the construction company, select the one with the name **About Us** at the bottom. Click on the **Import Template** button. After the importation is completed, start your editing.

(11) Move your cursor to any part of the page you want to edit, click on that part, delete what you do not want, add your own words, drag and drop pictures from your personal computer. After you finish with your editing, just save your work by clicking the **Publish** button at the bottom left corner of the page.

Building PROJECTS and NEWSROOM Pages

If you want to build the above pages, you are to follow the steps I took in the building of the other three pages. That will take you to end of the task. When you are choosing the Projects template, you can select any template from the library that shows projects achieved by any company. Edit it and upload your own pictures and words. At the end you are to click on **publish** to publish the page.

Also, you may look at the **PROJECTS** page of **Bechtel construction company** and see what they have there. On that page, the company has photos of some projects they have completed. The pictures are hyperlinked in a way that when you click on any of them, a post will open and tell you more about the project.

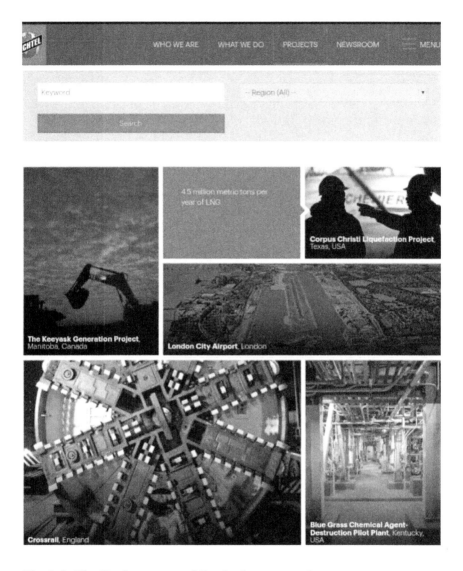

Fig 6.6: The Project page of Bechtel construction company

So, search for photo gallery template with elementor page builder, import it and use it to build the PROJECTS page of your construction company.

For the **NEWSROOM**, I recommend you type "**Blog**" when you get to the stage of choosing template. Choose any blog template you like from the list, edit, remove the module you don't like and click on **Publish/Update** after your design. With this guide, you will create the **NEWSROOM** page of the website.

Guide in Adding the Created Pages to main menu of the Construction Company Website

In a quick way, to add our created pages to the main menu of the construction company's website, take the steps:

Login to your WordPress admin area> Appearances> Menus> Navigation Menu or Main Menu> Click the boxes for the pages you want to add> Add to Menu> Arrange the pages in the way you want them to be using the drag and drop approach> Save Menu. With this quick guide, you will add the pages as main menu items.

Note: If "main menu" was not created by the default theme on the website, you have to create it first before adding the pages.

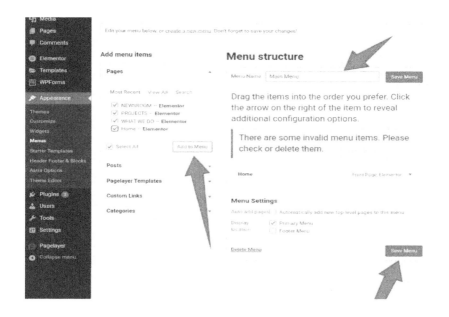

Fig 6.7: Selecting the already created pages to add to the main menu of my construction company Website

Other Things you can do on your Own on the Construction Company Website

Other things you can do on your own in the building of the construction company website is as follow:

- You can add the website title and
- Create social media links on the site

You can also give the site other small touches.

Chapter 7

Building Website with Elementor Pro 3.0 Beta

Elementor Plugin has been adding beauty to the look of websites created in the recent years. On June 7th, 2020, the company, Elementor, who name the plugin after their name, elementor, released a new version. The version was named Elementor Pro 3.0 Beta. The version came in the form of theme kit. You can do many things in one place with the new package.

In this chapter, I will be teaching you on how to build website using the new features of elementor pro plugin. I will explain some areas of the amazing theme builder. It is an easy to follow guide. It is going to be what you can do on your own after reading.

How to Access your Elementor Theme Builder

There are just few steps to take to access your elementor **Theme Builder** which is available in elementor 3.0 Beta. The theme builder is an all-in-one one design. It is like a folder containing many other files that you can use to make changes on your WordPress website.

To access the theme builder, take the following steps:

- Login to your WordPress dashboard
- Select Templates

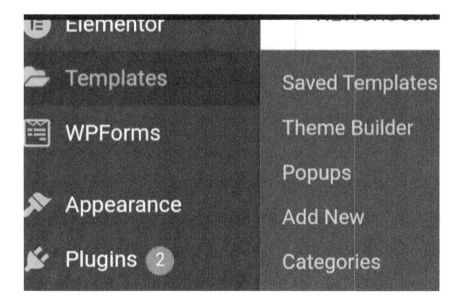

Fig 7: Accessing the theme builder of elementor pro 3.0 Beta

- Select Theme Builder

This simple guide is as shown in Fig 7

The Components of the Theme Builder

As you click on the **Theme Builder** as shown in Fig 7, you will see the component of the theme builder.

Fig 7. 1: The components of the elementor pro 3.0 theme builder

The components of elementor pro 3.0 Beta are:

- Header
- Footer
- Single Page
- Single Post
- Error 404
- Archive
- Products
- Products Archive and
- Search Results

Note: You may not necessarily work with all these components/templates in a site. Just choose any that suites the kind of website you are building and develop them. I will be taking you on gradual steps on how to use some of them to build your website.

Working with Single Page

Single page is used to build the page you want to have on your Website. When you click on this application, it opens and gives you the option to choose the template you want to use on the page. You can as well redesign the page and add your own pictures and texts.

After you are done with the editing, you can save the page and use it on another future page you want to build. With this development, you can even choose other existing pages you want the newly created page to replace and override. The single page you designed with the elementor template builder can even by used on every page of the site. You are given the option to choose where you want the change to be felt. You will master how to use it properly as time goes on.

How to Build a Website with Elementor Pro 3.0 Header

There are series of header templates available on elementor pro version. You are left with the option to choose any of the header templates from the **theme builder**, edit the way you want it to be and then upload it to any part of the page you want to use it on your website.

You can first design the header templates from the theme builder section and apply it to any part of your website you want it. To do that, take the following steps:

(1) Login to your WordPress dashboard
(2) Select **Templates** among the screen options
(3) Select **Theme Builder**
(4) Click on **Header**

Fig 7.2: The Header Template library section

(5) Click on **Add new header**

(6) Give the file a name

(7) Click on **Create New Template**

(8) Select any header template that you feel will be fine on the website you are building

Make sure that you are making this selection when the template library is under **Blocks** section

(9) Edit your selected header template to look good and fine

(10) Click on the Publish button at the bottom of the design environment

(11) Select the page which you want the header template to be applied to its header section or select for it to be used on the entire site if that is what you want

(12) Click on **Save and Close** button

Using this same guide, you can create Footer, Archive, Products, Products Archive and Search Results sections.

Note that you must not use all these sections on a website. It all depends on the kind of website you are building. Also, I want to inform you that **Archive** templates used to build archive section are best for news page.

Global Settings

To get to the global settings section, take these quick steps:

Settings Panel > Hamburger Menu > Global Settings

Under the global settings, you will see some actions you can take to make changes on different parts of the website.

The global settings of elementor pro 3.0 Beta is made up of some components. Among these components are:

- Global Color and
- Typography

In the Global Settings of the elementor 3.0 pro version, any change you make in that section affects your elements on the site. In this section, you can change the color that appears on your entire website. For example, you can give the background of you pages blue or pink color.

Topography has to do with the texts that are on the website. With this global setting, you can change your site font size and styling. Maybe you do not like the heading titles of the pages of your website, you can increase or decrease the size through this settings section. Also, you can decide to change the default font style to another. You can change the default font style to Times New Roman or any other from the initial one. You can play and experiment with this property.

How to Choose Static Home Page for Elementor Pro 3.0 Beta Design

To create static home page on elementor pro 3.0, these are what you need to do:

- Create your pages using elementor

Just as I have been teaching you on how to create pages using elementor, follow the same step and create pages choosing any template of your choice. These pages can be **Home, Posts, About Us, Contact, and Services.**

- Go back to your dashboard after creating the pages and start adding them as menu items
- Select **Settings** from the list of the screen options and then **Reading**

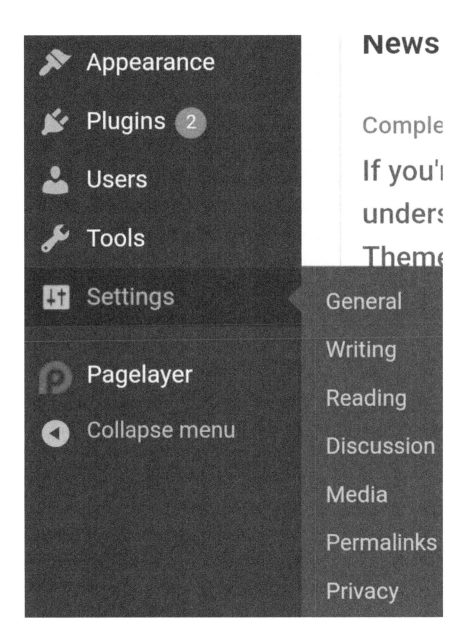

Fig 7.3: Select Settings followed by Reading

- As a new section opens when you selected Reading, at **Your homepage displays,** just tick the Static page option

113

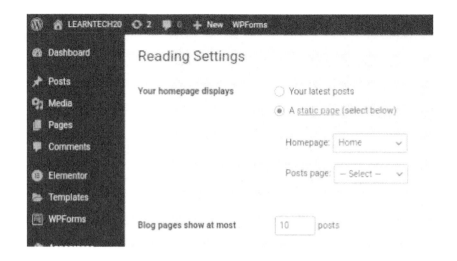

Fig 7.4: Choosing a static page

- From the drop down, select the page you want to use as your static page and click on **Save Changes** at the bottom part of the page

Note: By static page, I mean the page visitors will see first once they your website main link. For example, if a visitor visit the learning site www.learntech20.com, the page is where he or she will see first. So, apply these steps but there is another way to do this.

Author's Contact

You can reach me through my email: **michaelscott2020sm@gmail.com**